contents

NZ, Canada, US and UK readers
Please note that Australian cup and spoon
measurements are metric. A quick conversion
guide appears on page 63.

Essential nutrients

A balanced diet is made up of carbohydrates, dietary fibre, protein, fats, vitamins, minerals and water. The chart below focuses on a number of the essential dietary components that are commonly lacking in vegetarian diets – so make sure you include some or all of the following food sources in your diet.

Nutrient	Food sources for vegetarians
Protein	Grains and pulses, when eaten in tandem, provide adequate protein in a vegetarian diet – so have some of each every day. Grains: wheat, rice, oats, barley, rye, millet, maize (corn), buckwheat. Pulses: any dried beans (soy beans are particularly protein-rich), dried peas, lentils. Protein is also present in nuts and seeds (sesame, pumpkin, sunflower, etc) and in dairy products (milk, cheese, yogurt, etc).
Vitamin B12	Strict vegetarian diets lack vitamin B12, as its source is animal-based foods. The only vegetarian-friendly B12 options are: fortified soy drink, yogurt, milk, cheese and eggs. Alternatively, you can take a B12 supplement.
Iron	Vegetarians are commonly anaemic, caused by insufficient iron in their diets. Iron can be found in: iron-fortified breakfast cereals, spinach, silverbeet, broccoli, beans, lentils, dried fruit, cocoa powder and meat substitutes.
Calcium	Vegetarians who avoid dairy products can find calcium in these products: soy drink (fortified with calcium), Asian greens, silverbeet, spinach, almonds, brazil nuts, hazelnuts, tahini (sesame seed paste) and tofu.
Zinc	Primarily present in animal-based foods, zinc can also be found in: wholemeal and grain breads, pulses, nuts, and bran and wholegrain breakfast cereals.

Fat alert

While cutting meat from the diet can reduce a vegetarian's fat intake, it is important to recognise that fats are also present (and sometimes at high levels) in many foods commonly consumed by vegetarians. Don't fall into the trap of thinking that because you don't eat meat, you can have as much cheese as you like, for example. Vegetarian or not, a diet high in saturated fats should be avoided by all who are committed to good health. Of course, we all need some fats in our diet – but learn to choose your fat sources sensibly.

Sources of good fats include: olive and other vegetable oils, avocados, grains, nuts and seeds.

Sources of saturated fats include: butter, cream, milk, cheese, and coconut milk, cream and oil. Eat these foods in smaller quantities and less frequently.

Read between the lines

Strict vegetarians need to read food labels carefully when purchasing commercially packaged products as they can contain hidden ingredients derived from animals. Following are some terms to watch out for.

Animal fats are commonly used in the manufacture of biscuits, cakes and pastry so, unless the product label specifies it has been made from vegetable fats, don't buy it.

Rennet, which used to be made from the lining of calves' stomachs, separates the curds from the whey in cheesemaking. Today, most cheeses are made with a vegetable based rennet, but unless the label specifies this, you can't be sure.

Gelatine (or **gelling agents**) is made from animal hooves, hide and bones, as well as fish bones. This product is commonly found in savoury and sweet foods, but be especially careful with commercially made desserts and yogurts. The capsules used in vitamin supplements can also be made using gelatine.

mixed mushrooms with garlic chives

800g flat mushrooms
100g shiitake mushrooms
100g swiss brown mushrooms
150g oyster mushrooms
cooking-oil spray
¼ cup (60ml) red wine vinegar
1 tablespoon olive oil
2 cloves garlic, crushed
⅔ cup coarsely chopped fresh chives
2 cups loosely packed fresh flat-leaf parsley leaves
1 medium red onion (170g), sliced thinly

Preheat oven to slow.
Cut flat mushrooms coarsely into large pieces; combine with remaining mushrooms.
Spread mushrooms, in single layer, in two large shallow baking dishes; spray mushrooms with oil. Cook, uncovered, in slow oven about 40 minutes or until tender.
Heat vinegar, oil and garlic in small saucepan, stirring, 1 minute. Place vinegar mixture in large bowl with mushrooms, chives, parsley and onion; toss gently to combine.

serves 4
per serving 6.8g fat (0.8g saturated); 598kJ (143 cal); 9g carb
tip This recipe can be served warm or cold.

pan-fried tofu with cabbage salad

You need half a chinese cabbage for this recipe.

3 x 300g pieces fresh firm
silken tofu
1 tablespoon finely chopped
fresh lemon grass
2 fresh small red thai chillies,
sliced thinly
1 medium red onion (170g),
sliced thinly
1 cup (80g) bean sprouts
4 cups (320g) finely shredded
chinese cabbage
¾ cup firmly packed fresh
coriander leaves
sweet and sour dressing
⅓ cup (80ml) lime juice
2 teaspoons grated palm sugar
2 tablespoons soy sauce

Pat tofu all over with absorbent paper.
Slice each tofu piece vertically into
four slices. Place tofu slices, in single
layer, on absorbent-paper-lined tray;
cover tofu with more absorbent paper,
stand at least 10 minutes.
Meanwhile, make sweet and
sour dressing.
Cook tofu, in batches, in large
heated lightly oiled frying pan until
browned both sides.
Meanwhile, place remaining ingredients
in large bowl; toss gently to combine.
Divide salad among serving dishes;
top with tofu, serve with sweet and
sour dressing.
sweet and sour dressing Place
ingredients in small jug; whisk until
sugar dissolves.

serves 4
per serving 15.4g fat (2.3g saturated);
1221kJ (292 cal); 7.9g carb
tip This salad can be prepared
several hours ahead.

haloumi and grilled vegetable salad

2 medium red
  capsicums (400g)
2 medium yellow
  capsicums (400g)
1 medium eggplant (300g),
  sliced thickly
cooking-oil spray
2 cloves garlic, crushed
350g haloumi cheese,
  sliced thinly
1 tablespoon lemon juice
1 small red onion (100g),
  sliced thinly
100g baby rocket leaves
¼ cup loosely packed
  fresh basil leaves
½ cup (80g) drained
  caperberries, rinsed
1 lemon, cut into wedges
lemon dressing
⅓ cup (80ml) lemon juice
2 tablespoons olive oil
1 teaspoon sugar

Preheat grill. Quarter capsicums; discard seeds and membranes. Roast under grill, skin-side up, until skin blisters and blackens. Cover capsicum pieces with plastic or paper for 5 minutes; peel away skin, slice thinly.

Place eggplant slices on oiled oven tray; spray with oil, sprinkle with half of the garlic. Cook under preheated grill, turning occasionally, about 15 minutes or until softened. Cool 10 minutes; slice into thick strips.

Meanwhile, make lemon dressing.

Combine cheese in small bowl with juice and remaining garlic. Cook cheese in heated lightly oiled large frying pan until browned both sides.

Meanwhile, place capsicum, eggplant and dressing in large bowl with onion, rocket, basil and caperberries; toss gently to combine.

Divide salad among serving plates; top with cheese and lemon wedges.

lemon dressing Place ingredients in screw-top jar; shake well.

serves 4
per serving 25.7g fat (11g saturated); 1609kJ (385 cal); 14.6g carb
tip With the exception of the cheese, this recipe can be prepared several hours ahead; store, covered, in the refrigerator. Cook the cheese just before serving.

beetroot, pumpkin and spinach salad with fetta polenta

You need a small butternut pumpkin weighing about 1kg, unpeeled, for this recipe.

2 cups (500ml) water
2 cups (500ml)
  vegetable stock
1 cup (170g) polenta
200g fetta cheese, crumbled
10 small beetroots (600g)
2 tablespoons olive oil
700g peeled pumpkin,
  diced into 4cm pieces
150g baby spinach leaves
¾ cup (75g) toasted walnuts,
  chopped coarsely
walnut vinaigrette
2 tablespoons walnut oil
¼ cup (60ml) olive oil
¼ cup (60ml) lemon juice

Preheat oven to moderately hot. Grease 20cm x 30cm lamington pan; line with baking paper.

Combine the water and stock in large saucepan; bring to a boil. Add polenta, stirring constantly. Reduce heat; cook, stirring, 10 minutes or until polenta thickens. Stir in cheese then spread polenta into prepared pan. Cool 10 minutes then cover; refrigerate 1 hour or until polenta is firm.

Meanwhile, discard beetroot stems and leaves; quarter unpeeled beetroots. Place in large shallow baking dish, drizzle with half of the oil. Roast, uncovered, in moderately hot oven 15 minutes.

Add pumpkin, drizzle with remaining oil. Roast, uncovered, in moderately hot oven about 30 minutes or until vegetables are tender.

Meanwhile, make walnut vinaigrette.

When cool enough to handle, peel beetroot. Place in large bowl with dressing; toss gently to combine.

Turn polenta onto board; trim edges. Cut polenta into 12 pieces; cook, in batches, on heated oiled grill plate (or grill or barbecue) until browned both sides and heated through.

Add pumpkin, spinach and nuts to beetroot mixture; toss gently to combine. Divide polenta pieces among serving plates; top with salad.

walnut vinaigrette Combine ingredients in screw-top jar; shake well.

serves 4
per serving 58.8g fat (13.3g saturated); 3449kJ (825 cal); 52.2g carb
tip The polenta and dressing can be made a day ahead; store, covered, in the refrigerator.

sesame omelette and crisp mixed vegetable salad

You need about half a medium chinese cabbage for this recipe.

8 eggs
½ cup (125ml) milk
½ cup coarsely chopped
   fresh garlic chives
2 tablespoons toasted
   sesame seeds
8 cups (640g) finely shredded
   chinese cabbage
2 fresh long red chillies,
   seeded, sliced thinly
1 large red capsicum (350g),
   sliced thinly
1 large green capsicum (350g),
   sliced thinly
1 tablespoon coarsely
   chopped fresh mint
1 tablespoon finely chopped
   fresh lemon grass
sweet chilli dressing
2 teaspoons toasted
   sesame seeds
¼ cup (60ml) rice vinegar
¼ cup (60ml) peanut oil
1 teaspoon sesame oil
¼ cup (60ml) sweet chilli sauce

Whisk eggs in large jug with milk, chives and seeds until well combined. Pour a quarter of the egg mixture into heated lightly oiled wok or large frying pan; cook over medium heat, tilting wok, until omelette is just set. Remove from wok; repeat with remaining egg mixture to make four omelettes. Roll cooled omelettes tightly; cut into 3mm "wheels".
Make sweet chilli dressing.
Place three-quarters of the omelette in large bowl with cabbage, chilli, capsicums, mint, lemon grass and dressing; toss gently to combine.
Divide salad among serving plates; top with remaining omelette.
sweet chilli dressing Combine ingredients in screw-top jar; shake well.

serves 4
per serving 30.8g fat (7.2g saturated); 1718kJ (411 cal); 13.3g carb
tip The omelettes can be made up to 3 hours ahead and stored, covered, in the refrigerator; roll and slice just before assembling salad.

brown rice, chickpea and pepita salad with kumara-potato patties

1½ cups (300g) brown rice

1 large kumara (500g),
  chopped coarsely

4 small potatoes (480g),
  chopped coarsely

2 tablespoons plain flour

2 tablespoons sour cream

2 tablespoons finely chopped
  fresh chives

¼ cup (35g) plain flour, extra

2 tablespoons vegetable oil

300g can chickpeas, rinsed, drained

⅓ cup (55g) pepitas

⅓ cup (55g) raisins

3 trimmed celery stalks (300g),
  sliced thinly

2 tablespoons finely chopped
  fresh flat-leaf parsley

¼ cup finely chopped fresh mint

1 tablespoon finely grated
  lemon rind

1 medium red onion (170g),
  sliced thinly

3 small tomatoes (270g),
  chopped finely

tahini dressing

2 tablespoons tahini

½ cup (125ml) lemon juice

¼ cup (60ml) olive oil

Cook rice in large saucepan of boiling water, uncovered, until rice is tender; drain. Rinse under cold water; drain.

Meanwhile, boil, steam or microwave kumara and potato, separately, until tender; drain. Mash combined kumara and potato in large bowl; cool 10 minutes.

Make tahini dressing.

Stir flour, sour cream and chives into mashed kumara mixture. Using hands, shape mixture into eight patties; coat patties in extra flour. Heat oil in large non-stick frying pan; cook patties, four at a time, until browned lightly both sides and heated through. Cover to keep warm.

Place rice in large bowl with dressing and remaining ingredients; toss gently to combine. Serve rice salad with patties.

tahini dressing Combine ingredients in screw-top jar; shake well.

serves 4

per serving 42.6g fat (7.9g saturated); 4013kJ (960 cal); 121.1g carb

tip Pepitas, dried roasted pumpkin seeds, are easily found in most health food stores and supermarkets.

tuscan white bean salad

2 x 400g cans white beans, rinsed, drained
1 medium red onion (170g), chopped finely
⅔ cup (100g) drained semi-dried tomatoes
150g mozzarella cheese, cut into 1cm pieces
½ cup (75g) seeded kalamata olives
150g rocket
oregano balsamic vinaigrette
1 clove garlic, crushed
1 tablespoon finely chopped fresh oregano
¼ cup (60ml) balsamic vinegar
¼ cup (60ml) extra virgin olive oil

Combine beans, onion, tomato, cheese
and olives in medium bowl.
Make oregano balsamic vinaigrette.
Drizzle salad with vinaigrette; toss
gently to combine.
Serve salad with rocket.
oregano balsamic vinaigrette Combine
ingredients in screw-top jar; shake well.

serves 4
per serving 24.6g fat (7.6g saturated);
1526kJ (365 cal); 18.5g carb
tip Many varieties of already cooked white beans
are available canned, among them cannellini,
butter and haricot beans; any of these are
suitable for this salad.

vietnamese omelette

5 dried shiitake mushrooms

8 eggs

½ cup (125ml) milk

1 tablespoon finely chopped
fresh vietnamese mint

1 tablespoon peanut oil

5 green onions, sliced thinly

2 cloves garlic, crushed

230g can sliced bamboo
shoots, drained

1 medium carrot (120g),
sliced thinly

1 large red capsicum (350g),
sliced thinly

1 cup (80g) bean sprouts

1 tablespoon mild
chilli sauce

2 tablespoons light
soy sauce

1 tablespoon finely chopped
fresh coriander

Place mushrooms in small heatproof bowl;
cover with boiling water. Stand 20 minutes;
drain. Discard stems; slice caps thinly.

Meanwhile, whisk eggs, milk and mint in
medium bowl until combined.

Heat half of the oil in medium frying pan;
cook onion, garlic and bamboo shoots, stirring,
until onion softens. Add carrot and capsicum;
cook, stirring, until carrot is just tender. Add
mushrooms, sprouts, sauces and coriander;
cook, stirring, until heated through. Remove
from pan; keep warm.

Heat remaining oil in pan. Add a quarter of
the egg mixture; cook over medium heat,
tilting pan, until egg mixture is almost set.
Place a quarter of the vegetable mixture
evenly over half of the omelette.

Fold omelette over to enclose filling; slide
onto serving plate. Repeat with remaining
egg and vegetable mixtures.

serves 4

per serving 16.8g fat (4.9g saturated);
1124kJ (269 cal); 12.2g carb

tip We used vietnamese mint in this recipe,
a narrow-leated pungent herb, but you can
use whatever kind of mint is available.

pumpkin, spinach and fetta frittata

You will need to buy a piece of pumpkin weighing approximately 800g to make this recipe.

4 cups (640g) coarsely chopped pumpkin

1 large potato (300g), chopped coarsely

125g baby spinach leaves, chopped coarsely

200g fetta cheese, crumbled

¾ cup (90g) coarsely grated cheddar cheese

8 eggs, beaten lightly

1 small red onion (100g), sliced thinly

Preheat oven to very hot. Grease deep 23cm-square cake pan; line base and two opposite sides with baking paper.

Place pumpkin in large microwave-safe bowl, cover; cook on HIGH (100%), stirring halfway through cooking time, about 5 minutes or until just tender. Place potato in small microwave-safe bowl, cover; cook on HIGH (100%) 4 minutes or until just tender.

Combine pumpkin and potato in large bowl; add spinach, cheeses and egg, stir to combine. Transfer egg mixture to prepared pan. Top with onion.

Bake in very hot oven about 25 minutes or until firm. Stand 5 minutes before serving.

serves 4

per serving 30.6g fat (16.2g saturated); 2052kJ (491 cal); 20.4g carb

tip If you don't have a microwave oven, boil or steam pumpkin and potato, separately, until just tender; drain.

vegetable curry with yogurt

2 teaspoons vegetable oil
4cm piece fresh ginger
   (20g), grated
3 green onions, sliced thinly
2 cloves garlic, crushed
1 long green chilli,
   chopped finely
¼ teaspoon ground
   cardamom
1 teaspoon garam masala
1 tablespoon curry powder
1 teaspoon ground turmeric
2 medium green apples
   (300g), grated coarsely
1 tablespoon lemon juice
2 cups (500ml)
   vegetable stock
½ small cauliflower (500g),
   cut into florets
4 yellow patty-pan squash
   (100g), halved
2 small green zucchini
   (180g), sliced thickly
150g baby spinach leaves
200g low-fat yogurt

Heat oil in large saucepan; cook ginger,
onion, garlic, chilli, cardamom, garam masala,
curry powder and turmeric until fragrant.
Add apple, juice and stock; cook, uncovered,
5 minutes, stirring occasionally.
Add cauliflower, squash and zucchini;
cook, uncovered, until vegetables are just
tender. Remove from heat; stir spinach and
yogurt into curry just before serving.

serves 4
per serving 4.3g fat (1.1g saturated);
614kJ (147 cal); 17.2g carb
tip This recipe can be made a day ahead;
store, covered, in the refrigerator.

dhal with egg and eggplant

2 cups (400g) red lentils
2 teaspoons vegetable oil
1 medium brown onion (150g), chopped finely
1 clove garlic, crushed
2 teaspoons ground cumin
½ teaspoon cumin seeds
1 tablespoon tomato paste
1 litre (4 cups) water
2 cups (500ml) vegetable stock
1 large tomato (250g), chopped coarsely
3 baby eggplants (180g), chopped coarsely
4 hard-boiled eggs

Rinse lentils in large colander under
cold water until water runs clear.
Heat oil in large heavy-based saucepan;
cook onion, garlic, ground cumin, seeds
and paste, stirring, 5 minutes.
Add lentils with the water and stock; bring
to a boil. Reduce heat; simmer, uncovered,
about 40 minutes or until dhal mixture thickens
slightly, stirring occasionally.
Add tomato and eggplant; simmer, uncovered,
about 20 minutes or until dhal is thickened
and eggplant is tender, stirring occasionally.
Add whole eggs; stir gently until eggs are
heated through.

serves 4
per serving 10.7g fat (2.6g saturated);
1615kJ (395 cal); 42.8g carb

vegetable and tofu skewers

200g swiss brown mushrooms

1 medium green capsicum (200g), chopped coarsely

1 medium red capsicum (200g), chopped coarsely

1 medium yellow capsicum (200g), chopped coarsely

3 baby eggplants (180g), chopped coarsely

300g piece fresh firm silken tofu, diced into 3cm pieces

8 yellow patty-pan squash (200g), halved

100g baby rocket leaves

blue cheese dressing

50g blue cheese

2 tablespoons buttermilk

200g low-fat yogurt

1 small white onion (80g), grated finely

1 clove garlic, crushed

1 tablespoon finely chopped fresh chives

1 tablespoon lemon juice

Thread mushrooms, capsicums, eggplant, tofu and squash, alternately, onto skewers.
Cook skewers on heated lightly oiled grill plate (or grill or barbecue) until tofu is browned and vegetables are just tender.
Meanwhile, make blue cheese dressing.
Serve skewers on rocket; drizzle with dressing.
blue cheese dressing Crumble cheese into small bowl; stir in remaining ingredients.

serves 4
per serving 11.8g fat (4.2g saturated); 1070kJ (256 cal); 14.5g carb
tip The skewers and dressing can be prepared several hours ahead; store separately, covered, in the refrigerator.

risoni with mushrooms, zucchini and green onions

500g risoni
1 tablespoon olive oil
60g butter
500g zucchini, sliced thinly
300g button mushrooms, sliced thinly
2 cloves garlic, crushed
1 tablespoon coarsely chopped fresh oregano
1 tablespoon lemon juice
1 tablespoon red wine vinegar
200g green onions, sliced thinly
½ cup (40g) coarsely grated parmesan cheese

Cook pasta in large saucepan of boiling water, uncovered, until just tender.
Meanwhile, heat oil with half of the butter in large frying pan; cook zucchini, stirring, until tender and browned lightly. Add remaining butter with mushrooms, garlic and oregano; cook, stirring, 2 minutes then stir in juice and vinegar. Remove from heat; stir in onion and cheese.
Place zucchini mixture in large serving bowl with drained pasta; toss gently to combine.

serves 4
per serving 22.1g fat (11.1g saturated); 2796kJ (669 cal); 93.3g carb
tip Risoni, like orzo, is small rice-shaped pasta. It is great added to soups or baked as a casserole, and as good as rice when served as a main-course side dish.

cottage cheese lasagne

3 large red capsicums (1kg)
1 egg
500g cottage cheese
1 tablespoon olive oil
500g button mushrooms,
  sliced thinly
2 large zucchini (300g),
  sliced lengthways
700g tomato pasta sauce
6 fresh lasagne
  sheets (300g)
150g rocket, trimmed
¼ cup loosely packed
  fresh basil leaves
⅓ cup (40g) finely grated
  cheddar cheese

Quarter capsicums; remove seeds and membranes. Roast capsicum under grill or in very hot oven, skin-side up, until skin blisters and blackens. Cover with plastic or paper for 5 minutes; peel away skin, cut into thick strips.

Preheat oven to moderate (or reduce oven temperature to moderate).

Combine egg and cottage cheese in medium bowl.

Heat half of the oil in large non-stick frying pan; cook mushrooms, stirring, until soft. Remove from pan.

Heat remaining oil in same pan; cook zucchini, stirring, until browned all over. Remove from pan.

Spread a third of the pasta sauce into shallow 2-litre (8 cup) rectangular baking dish; top with a lasagne sheet. Top with a third of each of the capsicum, mushrooms, zucchini, rocket and basil, then another lasagne sheet. Repeat layering, starting with pasta sauce and ending with lasagne sheet. Spread cottage cheese mixture evenly over pasta; sprinkle with cheddar cheese.

Bake, uncovered, in moderate oven about 35 minutes or until heated through. Stand 15 minutes before serving.

serves 6
per serving 13.2g fat (5.5g saturated); 1906kJ (456 cal); 56.2g carb
tip The lasagne can be made a day ahead; store, covered, in the refrigerator.

ricotta and spinach stuffed pasta shells

Large pasta shells, also known as conchiglioni, are available from gourmet delicatessens; you can use 16 cannelloni shells instead.

32 large pasta shells (280g)
500g spinach
250g low-fat ricotta cheese
500g low-fat cottage cheese
600ml tomato pasta sauce
1 cup (250ml) vegetable stock
1 tablespoon finely grated parmesan cheese

Cook pasta in large saucepan of boiling water, uncovered, 3 minutes; drain. Cool slightly.
Preheat oven to moderate.
Boil, steam or microwave spinach until just wilted; drain. Chop spinach finely; squeeze out excess liquid.
Combine spinach in large bowl with cheeses; spoon spinach mixture into pasta shells.
Combine sauce and stock in oiled 2-litre (8 cup) ovenproof dish. Place pasta shells in dish; sprinkle with parmesan. Bake, covered, in moderate oven about 1 hour or until pasta is tender.

serves 4
per serving 10g fat (5.3g saturated); 2278kJ (545 cal); 71.3g carb
tip This recipe is best made just before serving.

roasted pumpkin and spinach risotto

500g pumpkin,
  chopped coarsely
2 tablespoons olive oil
1.25 litres (5 cups) water
1½ cups (375ml)
  vegetable stock
1 large brown onion (200g),
  chopped coarsely
2 cloves garlic, crushed
2 cups (400g) arborio rice
½ cup (125ml) dry
  white wine
250g spinach,
  chopped coarsely
½ cup (80g) toasted
  pine nuts
½ cup (40g) finely grated
  parmesan cheese
½ cup (125ml) cream

Preheat oven to hot.

Combine pumpkin and half of the oil in medium baking dish; roast, uncovered, in hot oven about 20 minutes or until tender.

Meanwhile, combine the water and stock in large saucepan; bring to a boil. Reduce heat; simmer, covered.

Heat remaining oil in large saucepan; cook onion and garlic, stirring, until onion softens.

Add rice; stir to coat rice in oil mixture. Add wine; cook, stirring, until liquid is almost evaporated. Stir in ½ cup simmering stock mixture; cook, stirring, over low heat until liquid is absorbed. Continue adding stock mixture, in 1-cup batches, stirring until absorbed after each addition. Total cooking time should be about 35 minutes or until rice is just tender.

Add spinach, nuts, cheese and cream to risotto; cook, stirring, until spinach wilts. Add pumpkin; stir gently into risotto.

serves 4
per serving 39.3g fat (12.4g saturated); 3390kJ (811 cal); 90.9g carb
tip This risotto is best made just before serving.

mushroom ragout with soft polenta

40g butter

2 large brown onions (400g),
  chopped coarsely

3 cloves garlic, crushed

¼ cup (35g) plain flour

400g button mushrooms

400g swiss brown
  mushrooms, quartered

400g flat mushrooms,
  sliced thickly

2 tablespoons tomato paste

⅔ cup (160ml) dry red wine

1.25 litres (5 cups) water

1 litre (4 cups)
  vegetable stock

2 teaspoons finely
  chopped fresh thyme

2 cups (340g) polenta

1 cup (250ml) milk

¼ cup (20g) finely grated
  parmesan cheese

Heat butter in large saucepan; cook onion and garlic, stirring, until onion softens. Add flour; cook, stirring, until mixture bubbles. Add mushrooms; cook, stirring, until mushrooms are just tender.

Add tomato paste and wine to mushroom mixture; bring to a boil. Reduce heat; simmer, uncovered, until liquid reduces by half. Add 2 cups of the water and half of the stock; return to a boil. Reduce heat; simmer, uncovered, 30 minutes. Stir in thyme.

Meanwhile, combine the remaining water and remaining stock in another large saucepan; bring to a boil. Add polenta; cook, stirring, until polenta boils and thickens. Add milk and cheese; cook, stirring, until cheese has melted. Serve mushroom ragout on polenta.

serves 8

per serving 7.5g fat (4.2g saturated); 1191kJ (285 cal); 38.4g carb

tip The ragout can be made a day ahead, but the polenta is best made close to serving.

barley and burghul fennel pilaf

Pearl barley is barley with the outer husk removed. It is available from major supermarkets and health food stores.

1 tablespoon olive oil
1 medium brown onion
   (150g), sliced thinly
2 cloves garlic, crushed
2 teaspoons caraway seeds
2 teaspoons ground cumin
2 teaspoons ground
   coriander
1½ cups (300g) pearl barley
2 cups (500ml)
   vegetable stock
2½ cups (625ml) water
1 cup (160g) burghul
2 medium red
   capsicums (400g)
40g butter
2 baby fennel (270g),
   trimmed, sliced thinly
⅓ cup (95g) yogurt

Heat oil in large saucepan; cook onion, garlic, seeds and spices, stirring, until onion softens.

Add barley; cook, stirring, 1 minute. Add stock and the water, bring to a boil; reduce heat, simmer, covered, 20 minutes.

Stir in burghul; cook, covered, about 10 minutes or until burghul and barley are tender.

Meanwhile, quarter capsicums, remove and discard seeds and membranes. Roast under grill or in very hot oven, skin-side up, until skin blisters and blackens. Cover capsicum pieces with plastic or paper for 5 minutes; peel away skin, slice thinly.

Heat butter in medium frying pan; cook fennel, stirring, until tender.

Just before serving, toss capsicum and fennel into barley mixture. Top with yogurt.

serves 4
per serving 16.8g fat (7.3g saturated); 2199kJ (526 cal); 77.5g carb
tip Regular barley can be used instead of the pearl barley.

couscous cakes with mediterranean vegetables

Couscous, a cereal made from semolina, is a North African staple.

1½ tablespoons olive oil
1 medium red onion (170g),
   sliced thickly
3 baby eggplant (180g),
   sliced thickly
2 medium green zucchini
   (240g), chopped coarsely
250g cherry tomatoes
250g yellow teardrop
   tomatoes
¼ cup (60ml) balsamic
   vinegar
1 clove garlic, crushed
1½ cups (300g) couscous
1½ cups (375ml)
   boiling water
¼ cup (20g) finely grated
   parmesan cheese
2 tablespoons coarsely
   chopped fresh basil
60g butter

Heat 2 teaspoons of the oil in large frying pan; cook onion, eggplant and zucchini, stirring, until vegetables soften.

Stir in tomatoes, vinegar, garlic and remaining oil; cook, stirring occasionally, about 10 minutes or until tomatoes are very soft.

Meanwhile, combine couscous with the water in large heatproof bowl; cover, stand 5 minutes or until water is absorbed, fluffing with fork occasionally. Stir in cheese and basil.

Heat half of the butter in large frying pan, press half of the couscous mixture into four egg rings in pan; cook until lightly browned on both sides. Carefully remove egg rings, then couscous cakes. Repeat using remaining butter and couscous mixture.

Serve Mediterranean vegetables with couscous cakes.

serves 4
per serving 21.7g fat (10.2g saturated); 2132kJ (510 cal); 63.9g carb
tip The couscous can be prepared a day ahead, but the cakes should be cooked just before serving.

vegetable tagine with olive and parsley couscous

You need a piece of pumpkin weighing approximately 600g for this recipe.

1 tablespoon olive oil
1 medium red onion (170g), sliced thinly
2 cloves garlic, crushed
1 teaspoon dried chilli flakes
1 teaspoon ground coriander
½ teaspoon ground turmeric
1 teaspoon cumin seeds
500g pumpkin, chopped coarsely
2 medium potatoes (400g), chopped coarsely
2½ cups (625ml) vegetable stock
300g can chickpeas, rinsed, drained
½ cup coarsely chopped fresh coriander
olive and parsley couscous
1½ cups (375ml) vegetable stock
1½ cups (300g) couscous
30g butter
1⅓ cups (200g) seeded kalamata olives
½ cup coarsely chopped fresh flat-leaf parsley

Heat oil in medium saucepan; cook onion, garlic and chilli, stirring, until onion softens. Add spices and seeds; cook, stirring, until fragrant. Add pumpkin and potato; stir to coat vegetables in spice mixture.

Stir in stock; bring to a boil. Reduce heat; simmer, uncovered, about 10 minutes or until vegetables are almost tender. Stir in chickpeas; simmer, uncovered, about 10 minutes or until vegetables are tender.

Meanwhile, make olive and parsley couscous.

Stir coriander into tagine. Divide couscous among serving plates; top with vegetable tagine.

olive and parsley couscous Bring stock to a boil in medium saucepan. Remove from heat; stir in couscous and butter. Cover; stand about 5 minutes or until liquid is absorbed, fluffing with fork occasionally. Stir in olives and parsley.

serves 4
per serving 14.3g fat (5.8g saturated); 2487kJ (595 cal); 95.2g carb
tip This recipe can be prepared a day ahead; store tagine and couscous separately, covered, in the refrigerator.

corn and zucchini fritters with salsa

50g butter, melted

½ cup (125ml) milk

¾ cup (110g) plain flour

2 eggs, beaten lightly

210g can creamed corn

2 medium zucchini (240g),
grated coarsely

vegetable oil, for
shallow-frying

salsa

3 medium egg tomatoes
(225g), chopped coarsely

2 medium avocados (500g),
chopped coarsely

1 small red onion (100g),
chopped coarsely

2 tablespoons lime juice

2 tablespoons finely
chopped fresh coriander

Combine butter, milk, flour and egg
in medium bowl; whisk until smooth.
Add corn and zucchini; mix well.

Heat oil in medium frying pan; cook
heaped tablespoons of batter about
2 minutes each side or until browned
both sides and cooked through. Drain
on absorbent paper. Serve with salsa.

salsa Combine ingredients in small bowl.

serves 4
per serving 54.4g fat (15.2g saturated);
2700kJ (646 cal); 29.2g carb
tips Keep the cooked fritters warm in
the oven until serving time.
If you're concerned about the fat count,
use a non-stick frying pan sprayed with
cooking-oil spray rather than shallow-frying
the fritters.

chickpea corn enchiladas

We used 16cm-round corn tortillas, which are packaged in cryovac. Unused tortillas can be frozen in freezer bags for up to three weeks.

1 tablespoon olive oil
1 small white onion (80g),
   chopped coarsely
1 clove garlic, crushed
1 teaspoon sweet paprika
½ teaspoon ground
   chilli powder
1 teaspoon ground cumin
400g can tomato puree
300g can chickpeas,
   rinsed, drained
1 tablespoon coarsely
   chopped fresh coriander
8 corn tortillas
1 small red onion (100g),
   chopped coarsely
1 medium tomato (190g),
   chopped coarsely
1 small avocado (200g),
   chopped coarsely
½ cup (60g) coarsely grated
   cheddar cheese
½ cup loosely packed, finely
   shredded iceberg lettuce

Heat oil in medium saucepan; cook onion and garlic, stirring, until onion softens. Add spices; cook, stirring, 2 minutes. Add puree, bring to a boil; reduce heat, simmer, stirring occasionally, 5 minutes. Add chickpeas and coriander; cook, stirring, until hot.

Soften tortillas in microwave oven on HIGH (100%) for 30 seconds.

Divide chickpea mixture and remaining ingredients among tortillas, fold enchiladas to enclose filling.

serves 4
per serving 19.6g fat (5.8g saturated); 1434kJ (343 cal); 29.7g carb
tip You can also soften tortillas by wrapping them in foil and heating them in a moderate oven for about 5 minutes or until hot.

lentil cottage pie

800g medium new
  potatoes, quartered
40g butter
1 medium brown onion
  (150g), chopped finely
1 clove garlic, crushed
415g can crushed
  tomatoes
1 cup (250ml)
  vegetable stock
1 cup (250ml) water
2 tablespoons
  tomato paste
⅓ cup (80ml) dry red wine
⅔ cup (130g) red lentils
1 medium carrot (120g),
  chopped finely
½ cup (60g) frozen
  peas, thawed
⅓ cup coarsely chopped
  fresh flat-leaf parsley

Preheat oven to hot.

Boil, steam or microwave potato until tender; drain. Mash in large bowl with half of the butter.

Melt remaining butter in medium deep frying pan; cook onion and garlic, stirring, until onion softens. Add undrained tomatoes, stock, the water, paste, wine, lentils and carrot; bring to a boil. Reduce heat; simmer, uncovered, 15 minutes, stirring occasionally.

Add peas and parsley; cook, uncovered, 5 minutes. Spoon lentil mixture into shallow 1-litre (4 cup) ovenproof dish.

Spread potato mash on top. Bake, uncovered, in hot oven 20 minutes. Stand pie 10 minutes before serving.

serves 4
per serving 9.7g fat (5.6g saturated); 1513kJ (362 cal); 49g carb
tip If you're not concerned with keeping the fat content of this dish low, you can stir ½ cup of finely grated parmesan cheese into the potato mash before baking the cottage pie.

free-form spinach and ricotta pie

Taking the Greek pie spanakopita as our inspiration, we've simplified the recipe by replacing the traditional fillo pastry with ready-rolled puff pastry.

200g spinach

2 tablespoons olive oil

1 medium brown onion (150g), chopped coarsely

1 clove garlic, crushed

2 teaspoons finely grated lemon rind

¼ cup coarsely chopped fresh flat-leaf parsley

¼ cup coarsely chopped fresh dill

2 tablespoons coarsely chopped fresh mint

1½ cups (300g) ricotta cheese

2 sheets ready-rolled puff pastry

Preheat oven to very hot.

Boil, steam or microwave spinach until just wilted; drain on absorbent paper. Squeeze out excess liquid.

Heat oil in small frying pan, add onion and garlic; cook until onion softens.

Combine spinach, onion mixture, rind, herbs and cheese in large bowl; mix well.

Oil two oven trays and place in oven about 5 minutes to heat. Place a sheet of pastry on each tray, divide spinach mixture between sheets, leaving a 3cm border. Using a metal spatula, fold pastry roughly over edge of filling.

Bake pies in very hot oven about 20 minutes or until pastry browns.

serves 4

per serving 36.8g fat (16.9g saturated); 2161kJ (517 cal); 32.7g carb

tip For best results, use a pizza tray with holes in the base – this will make it possible to cook the pastry evenly.

antipasto puff pastry tartlets

¼ cup (60ml) olive oil

2 cloves garlic, crushed

1 small red capsicum (150g), chopped coarsely

1 small yellow capsicum (150g), chopped coarsely

1 medium zucchini (120g), sliced thinly

2 baby eggplants (120g), sliced thinly

1 small red onion (100g), sliced thickly

100g semi-dried tomatoes

150g baby bocconcini cheese, halved

½ cup (40g) finely grated parmesan cheese

½ cup firmly packed fresh basil leaves

2 sheets ready-rolled puff pastry

⅓ cup (85g) tomato pasta sauce

2 tablespoons olive tapenade

Preheat oven to moderately hot.

Combine oil and garlic in large bowl. Add capsicums, zucchini, eggplant and onion; toss gently to coat vegetables in mixture.

Cook vegetables, in batches, on heated oiled grill plate (or grill or barbecue) until browned lightly and just tender; transfer to large bowl. Add tomatoes, cheeses and basil; toss gently to combine.

Cut pastry sheets in half; fold edges 1cm inward, place on oiled oven trays. Divide sauce among pastry pieces; top with vegetable mixture.

Bake, uncovered, in moderately hot oven about 15 minutes or until browned lightly. Serve tartlets topped with tapenade.

serves 4

per serving 44.3g fat (18.2g saturated); 2767kJ (662 cal); 46.5g carb

tip For best results, use a pizza tray with holes in the base – this will make it possible to cook the pastry evenly.

larb tofu

900g fresh firm silken tofu
peanut oil, for deep-frying
1 medium red onion (170g),
    chopped finely
½ cup coarsely chopped
    fresh coriander
1 tablespoon finely chopped
    fresh lemon grass
2 fresh small red thai
    chillies, sliced thinly
2 tablespoons lemon juice
1 teaspoon grated
    palm sugar
1 tablespoon soy sauce
½ teaspoon sambal oelek
8 small chinese cabbage
    leaves (360g)

Pat tofu with absorbent paper; chop coarsely. Spread tofu, in single layer, on absorbent-paper lined tray; cover tofu with more absorbent paper, stand at least 20 minutes.

Heat oil in wok or large saucepan; deep-fry tofu, in batches, until lightly browned. Drain on absorbent paper.

Combine tofu in large bowl with onion, coriander, lemon grass and chilli.

Combine juice, sugar, sauce and sambal in small jug; stir until sugar dissolves. Pour dressing over tofu mixture; toss to combine.

Serve tofu mixture spooned into individual whole cabbage leaves.

serves 4
per serving 27.8g fat (4.5g saturated); 1634kJ (391 cal); 6.8g carb
tip It is important that the tofu is as well drained as possible before it is deep-fried. If you have time, pat the piece of tofu with absorbent paper then place it in a strainer or colander that has been lined with absorbent paper and set over a large bowl. Weight the tofu piece with an upright saucer topped with a heavy can; allow to drain this way for up to 3 hours.

stir-fried eggplant and tofu

1 large eggplant (400g)
300g fresh firm silken tofu
1 medium brown
  onion (150g)
2 tablespoons peanut oil
1 clove garlic, crushed
2 fresh small red thai
  chillies, sliced thinly
1 tablespoon grated
  palm sugar
850g gai larn,
  chopped coarsely
2 tablespoons lime juice
⅓ cup (80ml) soy sauce
⅓ cup coarsely chopped
  fresh thai basil

Cut unpeeled eggplant in half lengthways; cut each half into thin slices. Place eggplant in colander, sprinkle with salt; stand 30 minutes.
Meanwhile, pat tofu all over with absorbent paper; cut into 2cm squares. Spread tofu, in single layer, on absorbent-paper-lined tray; cover tofu with more absorbent paper, stand at least 20 minutes.
Cut onion in half, then cut each half into thin even-sized wedges.
Rinse eggplant under cold water; pat dry with absorbent paper.
Heat oil in wok; stir-fry onion, garlic and chilli until onion softens. Add sugar; stir-fry until dissolved. Add eggplant; stir-fry 1 minute. Add gai larn; stir-fry until just wilted. Add tofu, juice and sauce; stir-fry, tossing gently until combined.
Remove from heat; toss basil through stir-fry.

serves 4
per serving 14.7g fat (2.4g saturated); 1012kJ (242 cal); 10.7g carb
tip It is important that the tofu is as well drained as possible before it is deep-fried. If you have time, pat the tofu piece with absorbent paper then place it in a strainer or colander that has been lined with absorbent paper and set over a large bowl. Weight the tofu piece with an upright saucer topped with a heavy can; allow to drain this way for up to 3 hours.

stir-fried vegetables and tofu in black bean sauce

450g hokkien noodles

300g fresh firm silken tofu

2 tablespoons peanut oil

1 medium eggplant (300g), cut into thin strips

1 medium carrot (120g), sliced thinly

1 medium red capsicum (200g), sliced thinly

230g can sliced water chestnuts, rinsed, drained

1 clove garlic, crushed

2 teaspoons grated fresh ginger

250g broccolini, chopped coarsely

500g choy sum, chopped coarsely

2 tablespoons kecap manis

½ cup (125ml) black bean sauce

Place noodles in large heatproof bowl; cover with boiling water. Use fork to separate noodles; drain.

Pat tofu all over with absorbent paper; cut into 12cm pieces. Spread tofu, in single layer, on absorbent-paper-lined tray; cover tofu with more absorbent paper, stand at least 20 minutes.

Heat half of the oil in wok or large frying pan; stir-fry tofu, in batches, until lightly browned. Drain on absorbent paper; cover to keep warm.

Heat half of the remaining oil in same wok; stir-fry eggplant until soft. Add carrot, capsicum and water chestnuts; stir-fry until vegetables are just tender, remove from wok.

Heat remaining oil in wok; stir-fry garlic and ginger until fragrant. Add broccolini and choy sum; stir-fry until vegetables are just tender.

Add noodles, sauces and eggplant mixture; stir-fry until heated through. Add tofu; toss gently to combine.

serves 6

per serving 11.6g fat (1.9g saturated); 1643kJ (393 cal); 53.5g carb

tip It is important that the tofu is as well drained as possible before it is deep-fried. If you have time, pat the piece of tofu with absorbent paper then place it in a strainer or colander that has been lined with absorbent paper and set over a large bowl. Weight the tofu piece with an upright saucer topped with a heavy can; allow to drain this way for up to 3 hours.

glossary

bamboo shoots tender shoots of bamboo, available in cans; drain and rinse before use.

bean sprouts also known as bean shoots; new growths of assorted beans and seeds.

beetroot also known as red beets; round root vegetable.

black bean sauce Chinese sauce made from fermented soy beans, spices and flour.

broccolini a cross between broccoli and chinese kale. Milder than broccoli, it is completely edible.

burghul also known as bulghur wheat; hulled steamed wheat kernels that are dried and crushed into grains.

butter use salted or unsalted (sweet) butter; 125g is equal to one stick of butter.

buttermilk sold in refrigerated dairy compartments in supermarkets. Commercially made similarly to yogurt.

caperberries fruit formed after the caper buds have flowered; pickled with stalks intact.

capsicum also known as bell pepper or, simply, pepper.

caraway available in seed or ground form.

cardamom available in pod, seed or ground form; sweetly rich, aromatic flavour.

cheese

blue: also known as blue vein; mould-treated cheeses that are mottled with blue veining.

bocconcini: walnut-sized baby mozzarella; spoils rapidly so must be kept refrigerated, in brine, for two days at most.

cheddar: common cow-milk "tasty" cheese; aged and hard.

cottage: fresh, unripened curd cheese with a grainy texture.

fetta: crumbly goat- or sheep-milk cheese with salty taste.

haloumi: firm, cream-coloured sheep-milk cheese matured in brine; tastes like a minty fetta.

mozzarella: soft cheese with low melting point.

parmesan: also known as parmigiano; hard, grainy cow-milk cheese.

ricotta: soft, white cow-milk cheese; made from whey, ricotta has a sweet flavour.

chickpea also called hummus, garbanzos or channa; round, sandy-coloured legume.

chilli available in different types and sizes. Wear rubber gloves when seeding and chopping fresh chilli as it can burn skin. Remove membranes and seeds to lessen the heat level.

green: unripened thai chillies.

sweet chilli sauce: mild, thin Thai sauce made from chillies, sugar, garlic and vinegar.

thai: small, medium-hot and bright red in colour.

chinese cabbage also known as peking or napa cabbage, wong bok or petsai. Elongated with pale green, crinkly leaves.

choy sum also known as pakaukeo or flowering cabbage; eaten stems and all. Has long stems, yellow flowers and green leaves.

coriander also known as pak chee, cilantro or chinese parsley; bright-green leafy herb.

couscous fine, grain-like cereal product; made from semolina.

cream, sour thick commercially cultured soured cream with minimum fat content of 35%.

cumin also known as zeera.

curry powder a spice blend; can include dried chilli, cumin, cinnamon, coriander, fennel, fenugreek, mace, cardamom and turmeric.

egg some recipes use raw or barely cooked eggs; exercise caution if there is a salmonella problem in your area.

eggplant also known as aubergine.

fennel also known as finocchio or anise.

flour, plain an all-purpose flour made from wheat.

gai larn also known as kanah, gai lum, chinese broccoli and chinese kale; stems are used.

garam masala a spice blend; can include cardamom, clove, cinnamon, coriander, fennel and cumin.

garlic chives also known as chinese chives.

ginger also known as green or root ginger; thick, gnarled root of tropical plant.

hokkien noodles fresh wheat noodles resembling thick, yellow-brown spaghetti.

kecap manis dark, thick, sweetened soy sauce.

kumara Polynesian name for orange-fleshed sweet potato.

lemon grass a tall, clumping, lemon-smelling and -tasting, sharp-edged grass; use the white lower part of the stem.

lentils dried pulses often named and identified by their colour.

mushroom

dried shiitake: also called donko or dried chinese mushrooms; rehydrate before use.

flat: large, flat mushrooms with a rich earthy flavour.

oyster: also known as abalone. Fan-shaped grey mushroom with subtle oyster flavour.

shiitake: fresh are also known as chinese black, forest or golden oak mushrooms.

swiss brown: light- to dark-brown with full flavour; also known as roman or cremini.

oil

peanut: pressed from peanuts; has high smoke point (capacity to handle heat without burning).

sesame: made from white sesame seeds; a flavouring rather than a cooking medium.

vegetable: any of a number of oils sourced from plants rather than animal fats.

walnut: pressed from walnuts.

olive tapenade thick paste of black olives, olive oil, capers, anchovies and herbs.

onion

green: also known as scallion or (incorrectly) shallot; an onion picked before bulb has formed, having long, green edible stalk.

red: also known as spanish, red spanish or bermuda onion.

palm sugar also known as jaggery, or jawa or gula melaka; made from sap of sugar palm tree. Usually sold in rock-hard cakes; use brown sugar as substitute if unavailable.

parsley, flat-leaf also known as continental and italian parsley.

patty-pan squash yellow to pale green in colour with a scalloped edge.

pearl barley barley with outer husk removed. Available from major supermarkets and health food stores.

pepita dried pumpkin seeds.

pine nuts also known as pignoli; small, cream-coloured kernel from pine cones.

polenta also called cornmeal; flour-like cereal made of dried corn (maize) sold ground.

pumpkin also known as squash.

raisin dried sweet grapes.

rice

arborio: small, round-grain rice well-suited to risottos.

brown: natural whole grain.

risoni small rice-shape pasta; very similar to orzo.

rocket also known as arugula, rugula and rucola; a peppery-tasting green leaf.

sambal oelek also known as ulek or oelek; a salty paste made from ground chillies and vinegar.

spinach also known as english spinach and, incorrectly, silverbeet.

tahini sesame seed paste.

thai basil also known as horapa; has smaller leaves than sweet basil, purplish stems and slight licorice taste.

tofu also known as bean curd; off-white product made from "milk" of crushed soy beans; comes fresh as soft or firm, and processed as fried or

pressed dried sheets. Silken tofu refers to manufacturing method of straining the soy bean liquid through silk.

tomato

cherry: also known as Tiny Tim or Tom Thumb; small and round.

paste: triple-concentrated tomato puree used as flavouring.

pureed: (not tomato paste). Substitute with fresh peeled and pureed tomatoes.

semi-dried: partially dried tomato pieces in olive oil.

teardrop: small yellow pear-shaped tomatoes.

tortilla thin, round unleavened bread; wheat and corn tortillas are available.

vietnamese mint pungent, peppery narrow-leafed member of the buckwheat family.

vinegar

balsamic: balsamic vinegars range in quality depending on the ageing process. The most costly are very pungent.

rice: colourless vinegar made from fermented rice. Also known as seasoned rice vinegar.

water chestnuts small, brown tubers with crisp, white, nutty-tasting flesh; available in cans.

yogurt we used plain, unflavoured yogurt, unless otherwise specified.

zucchini also known as courgette.

index

facts & figures

These conversions are approximate only, but the difference between an exact and the approximate conversion of various liquid and dry measures is minimal and will not affect your cooking results.

Note: NZ, Canada, US and UK all use 15ml tablespoons. Australian tablespoons measure 20ml. All cup and spoon measurements are level.

Measuring equipment
The difference between one country's measuring cups and another's is, at most, within a 2 or 3 teaspoon variance. (For the record, 1 Australian metric measuring cup holds approximately 250ml.) The most accurate way of measuring dry ingredients is to weigh them. For liquids, use a clear glass or plastic jug having metric markings.

How to measure
When using graduated measuring cups, shake dry ingredients loosely into the appropriate cup. Do not tap the cup on a bench or tightly pack the ingredients unless directed to do so. Level the top of measuring cups and measuring spoons with a knife. When measuring liquids, place a clear glass or plastic jug having metric markings on a flat surface to check accuracy at eye level.

Dry measures

metric	imperial
15g	½oz
30g	1oz
60g	2oz
90g	3oz
125g	4oz (¼lb)
155g	5oz
185g	6oz
220g	7oz
250g	8oz (½lb)
280g	9oz
315g	10oz
345g	11oz
375g	12oz (¾lb)
410g	13oz
440g	14oz
470g	15oz
500g	16oz (1lb)
750g	24oz (1½lb)
1kg	32oz (2lb)

We use large eggs with an average weight of 60g.

Liquid measures

metric	imperial
30 ml	1 fluid oz
60 ml	2 fluid oz
100 ml	3 fluid oz
125 ml	4 fluid oz
150 ml	5 fluid oz (¼ pint/1 gill)
190 ml	6 fluid oz
250 ml (1 cup)	8 fluid oz
300 ml	10 fluid oz (½ pint)
500 ml	16 fluid oz
600 ml	20 fluid oz (1 pint)
1000 ml (1 litre)	1¾ pints

Helpful measures

metric	imperial
3mm	⅛in
6mm	¼in
1cm	½in
2cm	¾in
2.5cm	1in
6cm	2½in
8cm	3in
20cm	8in
23cm	9in
25cm	10in
30cm	12in (1ft)

Oven temperatures
These oven temperatures are only a guide. Always check the manufacturer's manual.

	°C (Celsius)	°F (Fahrenheit)	Gas Mark
Very slow	120	250	½
Slow	140 – 150	275 – 300	1 – 2
Moderately slow	170	325	3
Moderate	180 –190	350 – 375	4 – 5
Moderately hot	200	400	6
Hot	220 – 230	425 – 450	7 – 8
Very hot	240	475	9

at your fingertips

These elegant bookcovers store up to 12 mini books and make the books instantly accessible.

And the metric measuring cups and spoons make following our recipes a piece of cake.

Book Holder
Australia and overseas: $8.95 (incl. GST).

Metric Measuring Set
Australia: $6.50 (incl. GST).
New Zealand: $A8.00.
Elsewhere: $A9.95.
Prices include postage and handling. This offer is available in all countries.

Mail or fax Photocopy and complete the coupon below and post to ACP Books Reader Offer, ACP Publishing, GPO Box 4967, Sydney NSW 2001, or fax to (02) 9267 4967.

Phone Have your credit card details ready, then phone 136 116 (Mon-Fri, 8.00am-6.00pm; Sat, 8.00am-6.00pm).

Australian residents We accept the credit cards listed on the coupon, money orders and cheques.
Overseas residents We accept the credit cards listed on the coupon, drafts in $A drawn on an Australian bank, and also UK, NZ and US cheques in the currency of the country of issue. Credit card charges are at the exchange rate current at the time of payment.

Photocopy and complete coupon below

☐ **Book Holder** ☐ **Metric Measuring Set**
Please indicate number(s) required.

Mr/Mrs/Ms _____

Address _____

_____

Postcode _____ Country _____

Ph: Business hours ( ) _____

I enclose my cheque/money order for $ _____ payable to ACP Publishing.

OR: please charge $ _____ to my ☐ Bankcard ☐ Mastercard

☐ Visa ☐ American Express ☐ Diners Club

Expiry date ____/____

☐☐☐☐ ☐☐☐☐ ☐☐☐☐ ☐☐☐☐
Card number

Cardholder's signature _____

Please allow up to 30 days delivery within Australia.
Allow up to 6 weeks for overseas deliveries.
Both offers expire 31/12/06. HLMVMM05

Food director Pamela Clark
Food editor Louise Patniotis
Nutritional information Amira Georgy
ACP BOOKS
Editorial director Susan Tomnay
Creative director Hieu Chi Nguyen
Senior editor Julie Collard
Designer Josii Do
Sales director Brian Cearnes
Publishing manager (rights & new projects)
  Jane Hazell
Marketing director Matt Dominello
Brand manager Renée Crea
Sales & marketing coordinator Gabrielle Botto
Pre-press Harry Palmer
Production manager Carol Currie
Chief executive officer John Alexander
Group publisher Pat Ingram
Publisher Sue Wannan
Editor-in-chief Deborah Thomas
Produced by ACP Books, Sydney.
Printing by Dai Nippon Printing in Korea.
Published by ACP Publishing Pty Limited,
54 Park St, Sydney;
GPO Box 4088, Sydney, NSW 2001.
Ph: (02) 9282 8618 Fax: (02) 9267 9438.
acpbooks@acp.com.au
www.acpbooks.com.au
To order books phone 136 116.
Send recipe enquiries to
Recipeenquiries@acp.com.au
Australia Distributed by Network Services,
GPO Box 4088, Sydney, NSW 1028.
Ph: (02) 9282 8777 Fax: (02) 9264 3278.
United Kingdom Distributed by Australian
Consolidated Press (UK), Moulton Park Business
Centre, Red House Road, Moulton Park,
Northampton, NN3 6AQ. Ph: (01604) 497 531
Fax: (01604) 497 533 acpukltd@aol.com
Canada Distributed by Whitecap Books Ltd,
351 Lynn Ave, North Vancouver, BC, V7J 2C4,
Ph: (604) 980 9852 Fax: (604) 980 8197
customerservice@whitecap.ca
www.whitecap.ca
New Zealand Distributed by Netlink Distribution
Company, ACP Media Centre, Cnr Fanshawe
and Beaumont Streets, Westhaven, Auckland.
PO Box 47906, Ponsonby, Auckland, NZ.
Ph: (9) 366 9966 ask@ndcnz.co.nz
South Africa Distributed by PSD Promotions,
30 Diesel Road, Isando, Gauteng, Johannesburg;
PO Box 1175, Isando, 1600, Gauteng, Johannesburg.
Ph: (27 11) 392 6065/7 Fax: (27 11) 392 6079/80
orders@psdprom.co.za

Clark, Pamela.
The Australian Women's Weekly
Vegetarian main meals

Includes index.
ISBN 1 86396 417 7

1. Vegetarian cookery. 2. Dinners and dining.
I. Title. II. Title: Australian Women's Weekly.

641.5636

© ACP Publishing Pty Limited 2005
ABN 18 053 273 546
This publication is copyright. No part of it may be
reproduced or transmitted in any form without the
written permission of the publishers.
Cover Chickpea corn enchiladas, page 47.
Stylist Yael Grinham
Photographer Rob Palmer
Home economist Liz Macri
Back cover at left, Cottage cheese lasagne, page 31;
at right, Haloumi and grilled vegetable stack, page 8.